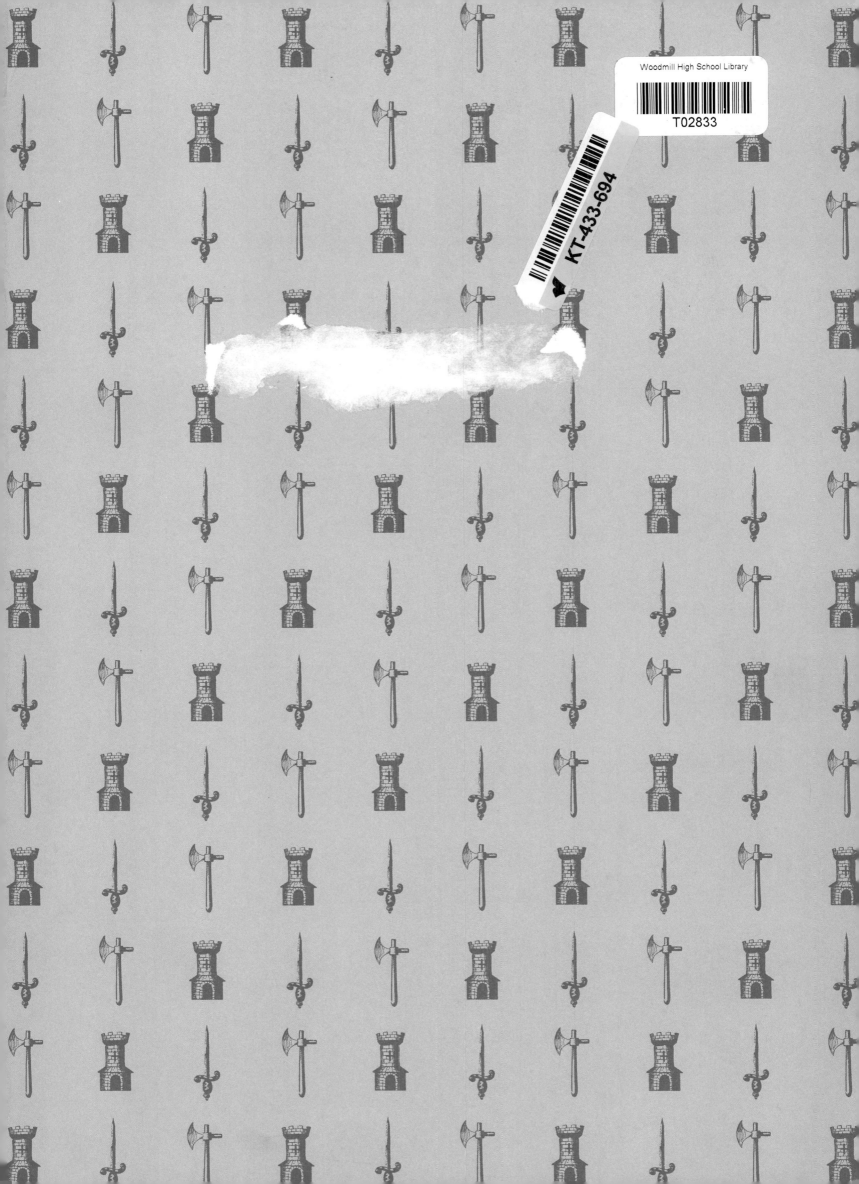

A SOLDIER'S LIFE

A Visual History of Soldiers through the Ages

Andrew Robertshaw

*"Soldiers, like other men, found more hard
work than glory in their calling."*

Frederic Remington

First published in Great Britain in 1997
by Heinemann Children's Reference,
an imprint of Heinemann Educational Publishers,
a division of Reed Educational and Professional
Publishing Limited,
Halley Court, Jordan Hill, Oxford, OX2 8EJ.

MADRID ATHENS FLORENCE PRAGUE
WARSAW PORTSMOUTH NH CHICAGO
SAO PAULO MEXICO SINGAPORE TOKYO
MELBOURNE AUCKLAND IBADAN
GABORONE JOHANNESBURG KAMPALA
NAIROBI

ISBN 0431 023018 (Hardback)
ISBN 0431 022922 (Paperback)

A CIP catalogue record for this book is available at the
British Library.

Printed in Hong Kong

Conceived and produced by Breslich & Foss, London
Series Editor: Laura Wilson
Editorial Assistant: Elizabeth Haylett
Art Director: Nigel Osborne
Design: Margaret Sadler
Photography: Miki Slingsby

CONTENTS

ROMAN SOLDIERS *c.*50 AD

Legionary Julius Favonius Facilus and Auxiliary Marcus Brigionus

At its height, the Roman Empire extended from southern Scotland to the Sahara Desert, and from Syria in the east to Spain in the west. It lasted more than one thousand years, and for most of that time, the Romans were fighting somewhere in the empire, either to gain new territory or to keep control of conquered territory.

The Roman army succeeded in this because it was very powerful and well organized. It consisted of nearly 30 legions, which were groups of 5,000 infantrymen and supporting cavalrymen. The legions were divided into groups of 80 to100 men, which were called centuries. Each century was divided into *contubernia*, or messes, which were groups of 8 soldiers who ate and slept together, sharing a tent, cooking equipment and rations.

BELOW: *Oil lamp and leather purse. In the first century AD, legionaries were paid 225 denarii (silver pieces) per year, and auxiliaries were paid 150 denarii.*

RECRUITMENT

Julius joined the army when he was 18. As a Roman citizen, he was able to become a legionary. Like all soldiers, Julius enlisted for 25 years. He could not marry during his service, but his pay was better than that of many civilians. When he retired, he was given land and money.

Marcus was not a Roman citizen but a Belgian, so he could only become an auxiliary *(see page 46)*, not a legionary. When he finished his service, Marcus and his children got Roman citizenship. Auxiliaries served abroad, in case they were more loyal to their own country than to Rome. They came from all over the empire: many who served on Hadrian's Wall came from Germany and France.

RIGHT: *Julius had* lorica segmentata *(jointed plate armour) over his tunic. Marcus wore mail armour.*

Soldiers on the march carried tools and cooking equipment as well as their weapons. Since they marched as much as 25 miles a day, their caligae *(hobnailed sandals) were a very important part of their equipment.*

RIGHT: *Marcus's belt with his protective bronze apron,* gladius *(short sword), and* pugio *(dagger) in its scabbard.*

FIGHTING

Roman soldiers were highly disciplined in battle. They formed ranks facing the enemy and threw their *pila* (javelins). Then, keeping in their ranks and protecting themselves with their shields, they fought with their swords.

The Romans developed military tactics for different situations. For example, if they were besieging a town, they formed a *testudo* (tortoise). A group of soldiers stood close together, with the men on the outside holding their shields at their sides and those in the middle holding their shields flat above their heads to protect them from above. In this way, all the soldiers defended one another, and provided they stayed in the formation, it was hard to stop them moving forward.

Roman army rations included grain, which one of the men in the contubernium *would grind into flour with a millstone, as well as cheese, meat, and vinegary wine.*

VIKING WARRIOR c.1000 AD

Herstein, Son of Asmund

Herstein wore linen trousers and two tunics, one linen and one woollen. Apart from his woollen cloak, these were the only clothes he took to war, and he was not able to change them for months. He used his cloak as a blanket at night.

Herstein had a shield, but because he was poor, his only weapons were an axe and a knife. When Viking warriors prepared for battle, they stood close together so that their shields overlapped and formed a wall to protect them from spears (see below).

LEFT: *In return for his service, Herstein received pay and the loan of a mail shirt, a helmet and two spears like the ones shown here. Soldiers were supposed to have as many as four spears and a sword, but most could not afford them. Swords were very expensive and not often used.*

In the summer of 1013 AD Herstein was preparing to join the army. Fifty years before, Herstein's grandfather had come to England from Denmark as part of a Viking raiding party. He decided to stay in England and make it his home. Herstein's grandfather was a heathen who believed in many different gods, but Herstein and his father, like most Vikings born in England, were Christian, and they spoke English, not Danish. Herstein still considered himself a Viking, though his loyalty was to the leader of his village. He chose Herstein to fight in the Anglo-Saxon army of the English king, Ethelred, against a new invasion of heathen Vikings from Denmark.

Herstein was a farmer, but everyone expected him to become a warrior when necessary and join the others chosen to march north to fight. Although Herstein was 30 years old, he had not fought before, so he hoped that there would be time for him and the other men to practise using their weapons before the battle started. Although he was worried by his lack of fighting experience, he was pleased to have the chance to gain honour and respect by serving the leader of his village.

ABOVE: Herstein took his most important possessions to battle with him. Like many Vikings, he enjoyed gambling, and kept his dice in the leather box. He kept his money in a leather purse. Many things cost less than one penny, so some of the coins were cut into halves and quarters. Herstein used the whistle to call his dog, Grighund, who followed him to battle.

FOOD

Herstein did not carry breakable pottery cups and jars with him, but he took ash wood bowls and cups. He used the knife for farm-work and to eat with, and he also used it as a weapon. Herstein had to find his own food, but he could trap birds, like this duck *(above right)*, and make a porridge from oats, rye and barley.

Herstein in full battle dress. His cloak was fastened with a silver brooch.

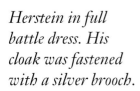

LIGHTING FIRES

Fire-lighting equipment (left). *To produce a flame, Herstein held a flint in one hand and struck it on the edge of a piece of steel so that sparks fell onto a piece of dry horse hoof or tinder fungus. When this began to glow, Herstein touched it with some linen, which burst into flame.*

THE NORMAN CONQUEST 1066

Drogo FitzPoyntz (Knight) and Robert, son of John (Archer)

In 911, the French king gave some land to the Vikings in order to prevent them from attacking his territory. They settled in France and became known as Northmen or Normans. The part of France where they lived was called Normandy. Like all Vikings who settled abroad, they took up local ways, names, and the language, but they continued to invade other countries in order to gain more land.

The English king, Edward the Confessor, had promised his throne to his Norman cousin, Duke William. However, when Edward died in 1066, Harold Godwinson, a Saxon, was crowned. William's invasion force of over 7,000 men and horses sailed from France to claim the throne. They met the Saxon army at Hastings, and in the battle that followed, Harold was killed, and William was crowned king.

ABOVE: *Coloured braid for a knight's tunic.*

DUKE WILLIAM'S INVASION FORCE

Duke William's invasion force was made up of Norman knights, their followers and mercenaries. Many knights, like Drogo FitzPoyntz *(shown opposite right)*, had no land of their own in Normandy, but they knew that if William became king of England, he would reward them with Saxon land.

Mercenary soldiers like Robert *(shown opposite left)* were given money if a battle was won. When the Normans landed in England, Robert and the other mercenaries heard that food supplies were low, and they threatened to leave. William knew that he could not win without them, so he ordered that double rations be given to each man, even though there was little food left. This was a good idea, as the mercenaries stayed and the Normans won the battle and took as much food as they wanted from the defeated Saxons.

ABOVE LEFT: *There were different arrowheads for different targets: narrow-headed ones were used in battle because they could pierce mail, whereas arrows with broader heads were occasionally used against warhorses in battle but were mainly used for hunting. Men called fletchers made the fletchings on the ends of arrows out of goose feathers.*

The Normans brought food with them, but they also plundered Saxon farms and villages to feed themselves and their horses.

RIGHT: *Although Saxons hunted with bows and arrows, they did not fight with them. Norman armies included both crossbowmen and archers like Robert (shown opposite), who could shoot six or seven arrows per minute. They wore thick, padded tunics for protection.*

Drogo FitzPoyntz in full armour.
Knights like Drogo wore mail
and fought on horseback. The
Saxons, like the Vikings,
defended themselves with a
shield wall. Once it was
broken, the Normans
were able to defeat them.

SHOOTING AN ARROW·

Robert
strung his
bow with a
bowstring.

He drew an
arrow. Archers
either kept
arrows in a
quiver (shown
here) or stuck
them through
their belts or into
the ground.

He fitted the
arrow's nock
(groove) onto
the bowstring.

He aimed and
drew the
bowstring back
before shooting the
arrow.

RIGHT: Drogo's main
weapon was a sword.

THE THIRD CRUSADE 1191-92

Nicholas d'Artois (Knight) and William Trussel (Crossbowman)

The crusades began in 1095, when Pope Urban II called on Christians to capture the Holy Land (now Syria and Israel) from the Muslims. He was particularly intent on capturing Jerusalem, the city where Jesus was crucified. There were two major crusades during the next 60 years, and Jerusalem was captured, and then lost to Muslim forces. In 1190 Pope Gregory VIII preached a Third Crusade, and Frederick I Barbarossa, Emperor of Germany; Philip II of France and Richard I of England (known as Richard the Lionheart) raised armies and set out for the Holy Land. Many different types of people accompanied them on crusade, from rich knights such as Nicholas d'Artois, who travelled with their servants, to poor craftsmen, who had sold everything they owned in order to raise money for the journey.

FIRING A CROSSBOW

The cross-bowman strung his bow.

He fixed the string in a nock, which was linked to a trigger.

He slid the crossbow bolt into its groove.

He aimed at the target and pulled the trigger to shoot the bolt.

MOTIVES

The Pope had promised that all the crusaders' sins, past and future, would be forgiven. At this time, people's belief in God was strong, and the thought that they could be free to behave as they liked without fear of going to hell was very tempting. Although some people went on crusade for religious reasons, others, like Nicholas d'Artois, wanted adventure and the chance to acquire more land and treasure. In Europe, land always passed from one eldest son to another, and younger sons with no land often became crusaders in the hope of getting some. William Trussel, the crossbowman, is one of a number of men travelling with Nicholas, who is paying for him to go on crusade as one of his soldiers.

William (below) and Nicholas (right). Nicholas had cloth in the shape of a cross on his cloak to show that he was a crusader.

RIGHT: *Nicholas went into battle on horseback and fought with his lance, sword and axe.*

Nicholas's helmet covered his whole face. It had slits so that he could breathe, but he could only see what was in front of him.

ON THE MARCH

Like most crusaders, Nicholas and William had little idea of how far away the Holy Land was or what it was like. Knights like Nicholas, who wore mail, helmets and heavy cloaks, found them unbearable in the heat of the Holy Land, and many had sold or thrown away their armour before they reached Jerusalem. Poorer crusaders had little money to buy food, and many died of starvation, exhaustion or disease before they reached the Holy Land. If they travelled on foot, they also risked falling behind the mounted crusaders and being killed by Muslim soldiers. However, many of the men on the Third Crusade were well-armed, experienced soldiers like Nicholas and William. Richard I made the unarmed men travel in the middle of them, where they were protected by the armed foot soldiers and mounted knights.

RIGHT:
Rich men like Nicholas had enough money for food, and to pay for their horses to be shod and their armour mended, but like all the crusaders, they were at the mercy of the traders who travelled with them and charged high prices for their goods.

WARS OF THE ROSES 1455-85

Sir Thomas Burgh (Man-at-Arms), Richard Calle (Archer), and Edmund Clere (Billman)

The two most powerful families in England, both of whom had a legal claim to the throne, fought for more than 30 years over who should rule. These battles are now called the Wars of the Roses because one side, the House of Lancaster, had a red rose as its symbol, and the other side, the House of York, had a white rose. The Wars of the Roses eventually came to an end when Tudor defeated the Yorkist King at the battle of Bosworth in 1485. Richard III was killed in the battle, and Henry Tudor was crowned King Henry VII. Sir Thomas Burgh was a supporter of the House of York. He was a Knight Bannerette, with special permission to display his own banner (flag) when he went into battle. Like some Yorkists, Sir Thomas had to change sides quickly after the battle of Bosworth, but he was luckier than many because he found favour with the new king. A lot of Yorkist noblemen had their money and land taken away, and some were executed or sent into exile.

RIGHT: *Sir Thomas with two of his soldiers, Richard Calle, an archer (kneeling) and Edmund Clere, a billman (standing).*

ABOVE: *Sword and arrows. There were different arrowheads for different targets (see page 8). Knights like Sir Thomas Burgh did not usually fight on horseback but rode to the battlefield, then dismounted and fought on foot. There was not much fancy swordplay in the thick of battle – soldiers simply tried to slash or beat their opponents to death with any available weapon.*

WEAPONS

Battles began with a bombardment of arrows. The bow and arrow was the chief weapon for poor men, and there were more archers in the army than any other type of soldier. As well as arrows, there were also cannons and handguns although these were very crude, with matchlock mechanisms *(see page 15)*. They were, however, very popular with noblemen like Sir Thomas Burgh, who spent large amounts of money buying as many guns as they could.

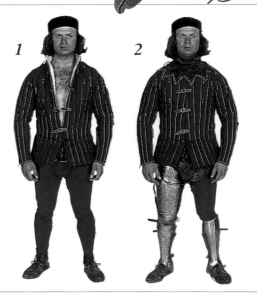

ARMOUR

A suit of armour was known as a harness and a man who wore one was called a man-at-arms. There were no high-quality armourers (armour makers) in England at this time, so armour was imported from Italy and Germany. Arms fairs were held in Europe, where armour and weapons could be bought. This is how a suit of armour was worn:
1 An arming doublet *was worn to make the armour more comfortable.*

2 Greaves *were worn on the shins,* poleyns *on the knees,* cuisses *on the thighs, as well as* mail braies *(like shorts). A* mail standard *was worn around the neck.*
3 The breastplate *covered the chest and* besagues *protected the armpits.*
4 Upper and lower cannons *protected the arms, with* couters *on the elbows.*
5 Pieces of shoulder armour were called pauldrons. *An* arming cap *made the helmet more comfortable.*

RIGHT: *Edmund has Sir Thomas's pole axe. It was used for clubbing enemies. His own weapon is a bill – a pole with a hook for pulling knights off their horses.*

RAISING ARMIES

At the time of the Wars of the Roses, the law said that all men must own as much armour and weapons as they could afford and be prepared to serve their county as soldiers for 40 days every year. Noblemen, like Sir Thomas Burgh, were asked to provide a certain number of soldiers to serve the king, many of whom were their servants. Edmund was one of Sir Thomas's cooks. He wears a *jakke*, which was a jacket made of as many as 30 layers of linen, which acted as padding. *Jakkes* prevented arrow wounds, and were the cheapest and most common form of armour. The bowl-like object hanging from Edmund's belt is a buckler. These were worn as small shields to protect the hands, but they could also be used to hit people.

Richard Calle owned a small piece of land near Sir Thomas's estate. In return for protection against his enemies, Richard agreed to fight for Sir Thomas whenever it was necessary. He is wearing woollen hose (leggings), a mail shirt, and a jacket with Sir Thomas's livery (colours) of blue and white.

3

4

5

RIGHT: *Full armour, including a* sallet *(helmet) and* gauntlets *(armed gloves). A* bevor *covered Sir Thomas's chin and throat. The visor of the helmet could be pulled down to protect his eyes (below).*

CIVIL WAR NICKNAMES

The nickname "cavalier" comes from the Spanish *caballero*, meaning mounted soldier. The name suggested that the person was foreign, and royalist soldiers found this insulting. Parliamentarians were called "round-heads". This suggested that they were apprentices, who wore short hair. Men on both sides wore long hair, and it was rude to call a man a "round-head" because it meant that he was a worker of low status.

FOOD

The daily ration of "marching food" was one pound of round, hard biscuits or bread and one pound of either cheese or meat to eat with them. Soldiers were given knapsacks to carry their food but had to supply their own plates and cutlery.

Nehemiah was a tradesman and a supporter of Parliament who volunteered to join the army. His coat and shoes were issued to him, but he had to supply the rest of his uniform himself. Over his shoulder he wore an orange sash to show his support for the Earl of Essex. If he had not worn this, it would have been impossible to tell him from a Royalist sergeant.

ENGLISH CIVIL WAR 1642-49
Sergeant Nehemiah Wharton (Parliamentarian)

A civil war is a war between different groups of people within the same nation. This war broke out because the Royalists and the Parliamentarians had different views about the government and religion of England. The Parliamentarians felt that the king should have less power and Parliament more. The Royalists supported the king, Charles I. They claimed that he had been chosen by God to rule, as had his father, James I, before him. Like most of England, Charles I was Protestant, his queen, Henrietta Maria, was Catholic, and many people were suspicious that he preferred Catholics and foreigners to English people. The Parliamentarians thought that English people should be Protestant. The Civil War broke out after the Parliamentarians had Charles I's chief minister executed and the king tried to arrest five of the leading Parliamentarians.

RIGHT: *This gun is a matchlock musket. The match (a piece of rope boiled in saltpetre) was lit and applied to the priming powder so that the gun could be fired. However, the match often went out when it rained. Muskets were heavy and usually placed on rests for firing, like the one shown.*

RIGHT: *A halberd, which was a spear fitted with an axe head, with a sword and scabbard.*

THE NEW MODEL ARMY

When the Civil War broke out, there were fewer than 500 trained soldiers in England, so thousands of civilians were either encouraged or forced to enlist. Nehemiah Wharton volunteered to join the regiment of Denzil Holles, an MP (Member of Parliament). Many regiments were led either by MPs or by lords. The Parliamentary army was led by Robert Devereux, Earl of Essex, whose orange sash Nehemiah wore *(see opposite)*.

The New Model army was created in the spring of 1645 for two reasons. The first was to defeat the Royalist forces – which happened at the battle of Naseby in June 1645. The second was to establish an army with professional officers, rather than lords or MPs commanding the men, and with regular pay for all the soldiers. The New Model army was commanded by Sir Thomas Fairfax and his second-in-command, Oliver Cromwell *(shown top centre)*.

Richard (seated) at the end of a day's travelling. The infantry could travel roughly eight miles a day, and the cavalry 12 miles. At night, the infantry stayed in towns and villages, but the cavalry had to camp wherever they could find food and water for their horses, which was often far out in the country. Everyone had to meet the next morning before they could move on again, so progress was slow.

Soldiers often had haircuts to prevent lice from nesting in their hair.

Richard had soldier servants, who looked after him and his horses. The more important an officer was, the more servants he had. Generals travelled around in carriages with their wives.

ENGLISH CIVIL WAR 1642-49

Captain Richard Atkyns (Royalist)

Many friends and families found that they were fighting each other during the Civil War. Some people were confused because, although they supported the cause of Parliament, they felt it was their duty to be loyal to the king.

Parliamentarians with very strict religious views were called Puritans. They lived very simply and did not approve of dancing and fancy clothes. They even considered paintings and statues in churches to be wicked, because they thought that people would worship the images instead of worshipping God. However, not all Parliamentarians thought that enjoyment was sinful, and both Richard Atkyns and Nehemiah Wharton would have welcomed the chance to smoke a pipe and have a game of chess on a travelling set like this one (left).

After winning at the battles of Marston Moor (1644) and Naseby (1645), the New Model army seized King Charles I, and in 1649 they executed him. Although his son King Charles II raised an army, it was defeated by the Parliamentarians.

RIGHT: *A horseman's weapons were a sword and two pistols. This is a wheel-lock pistol. When it was fired, the wheel spun round and struck against a piece of stone, so that sparks ignited the powder.*

FIGHTING

At the start of a big battle, the two armies faced each other on the field. Usually, the infantry was in the middle of the line, with cavalrymen like Richard and his troopers positioned on either side of them. First, the cannons were fired, and then the cavalry charged, hoping to scatter the enemy cavalry and chase them away. If the cavalry were well disciplined, they would then turn round and attack the enemy infantry from behind.

While the cavalry were fighting, the infantry would begin to advance, firing their muskets. The aim of Nehemiah and the other infantrymen was to break up the enemy line before they engaged in hand-to-hand combat. For this they used the points of their pikes; then they fought with swords and the butts of their guns, which they used as clubs. Sometimes they fought until they were all either dead, wounded or exhausted, but if neither side managed to chase the other from the field, both sides claimed victory, although neither had really won.

LEFT: *Richard Atkyns was a country gentleman. When the war broke out, he used his own money to arm 60 cavalry troopers and led them into battle in Prince Maurice's Regiment of Horse. When he went into battle, he wore a helmet, buff-coloured coat, breeches and bucket-top boots. This was the same as the uniform of a Parliamentarian captain, and in spite of the red sash he wore around his waist, Richard could easily be confused with one. He arranged with the other Royalist soldiers to wear a bunch of leaves tucked in his helmet, so that they would always recognise him in battle and wouldn't attack him by mistake.*

AMERICAN INDEPENDENCE 1775-83

Private James Boswell and Sergeant Richard Laird (American)

In the 18th century, Britain founded colonies on the east coast of America. Known as the thirteen colonies, they were ruled by Britain and paid taxes to the British government. In the 1760s, colonists like James Boswell and Richard Laird were angered by demands for higher taxes, especially as they were not represented in the British Parliament. In 1775, war broke out between the colonists and the British troops. Unlike the British soldiers *(see page 20)*, colonists such as James and Richard were not professional soldiers but farmers and tradesmen with no experience of fighting.

Although the British won some early battles, they lost many men and found it difficult to recover from these early losses. The colonists went on to win important victories at Princeton and Saratoga (1777). The colonists' final defeat of the British at Yorktown in 1781 led to recognition of the colonists' independence and their new name – the United States of America.

Soldiers on both sides plaited their hair or tied it back in a pigtail. For parades, they greased their hair with fat and covered it with flour or white powder.

Compared to the British soldiers (see page 20) James was issued with very little equipment: a musket, cartridge box, bayonet, belt and coat. He had to supply his own shirt, breeches, socks and shoes.

ABOVE: *James's tinderbox. The glass on the lid of the box could be held up to the sun with a piece of newspaper or tinder (see page 7) beneath it. The action of the sun on the glass made the newspaper heat up, and after a while it caught fire.*

James's coat was known as a lottery coat. There was often a shortage of uniforms during the war, and a lottery would be held among the soldiers to see who would get them.

THE CONTINENTAL ARMY

At the start of the war, the colonists did not have an army. Instead, they had a system by which any man between the ages of 16 and 60 could be asked to serve for short periods of time in the state militia, using weapons brought from home. Although these men fought bravely, they did not have proper training or discipline. It soon became clear to George Washington, their commander in chief, that the colonists needed a regular army. In 1776, he persuaded Congress to raise a Continental Army, for which each state had to provide a number of soldiers. James Boswell joined up in June 1776.

EATING AND SLEEPING

Soldiers were divided into units of five or six men who ate together and shared a tent. They were called messmates. Each group of messmates was given an iron cooking pot, which they hung over a fire. There were no official army cooks. The man who was the best cook in the group usually had the job of preparing supper, which was often a stew made out of rations and anything else available. The cooking pots were very heavy and were often thrown away by soldiers on a long march.

In order for all the men to fit into the tent, they lay across its width. The most senior soldier slept at the back of the tent, so that he would not be interrupted as the other men got up to take their turn at guard duty during the night.

CLOTHING

Richard Laird (left) wore a cap made of boiled leather with a horsehair crest. He needed new breeches, but because of the shortages he had to wear his old ones until they fell apart. He wore spatterdashes (gaiters) to prevent his shoes getting wet.

James Boswell's cartridge box, his powder horn, which is marked with his name, and a brush for cleaning his musket after he has fired it.

When a flintlock weapon was fired, the flint struck the frizzen (the L-shaped piece in front of it), to make a spark. This ignited the powder in the pan (see page 21) and caused the powder inside the gun to explode, firing the ball out of the muzzle.

Corporal Naylor and Private Fell in full marching order, ready to go on campaign. Soldiers were known as redcoats because of their red uniform jackets. All soldiers wore black felt cocked hats trimmed with lace and a regimental button. Around the soldiers' necks were stocks, which kept their heads up and were very uncomfortable.

FOOD

Basic British military rations *(below)* were bread, cheese, and meat, which had to be cooked by the soldier himself. Sometimes, there was an issue of rice, oats, or even vegetables, which could be used to make a stew. Although he risked a flogging if he was caught, James stole potatoes, carrots, and corn *(above)* from nearby fields. He carried water in a wooden canteen, although it was not really safe to drink, and soldiers were often given beer or tea instead.

Inside every soldier's knapsack was a spare shirt to wear on Sundays, a blanket, food and personal items such as a shaving brush and penknife.

RIGHT: *Shoes did not have left and right feet. The soldiers reversed them each day.*

AMERICAN INDEPENDENCE 1775-83

Corporal George Naylor and Private James Fell (British)

20238
355

Like many soldiers, James Fell was a farm labourer before he joined the 47th Regiment of Foot. One autumn, when the harvest was finished, James could not find any work, but then he met Corporal Naylor and decided to join the army. When war broke out in America, James was told that his regiment would have to go there. The reason for the fighting was that America, then a British colony, wanted to be independent, and Britain wanted to continue governing it. James did not want to travel 3,000 miles from home, spending about three months in the hold of a sailing ship, and he thought of running away, or deserting. But then he had to watch while a soldier who had deserted and been caught was given 500 lashes with a whip called a cat-o'-nine-tails. James decided that going to America was better than risking such a flogging.

FIGHTING

Soldiers on both sides began the battle by firing at each other and then charged with bayonets. Neither side was able to aim their guns accurately if the target was more than 100 yards away, so they waited until the enemy was as close as possible before firing. British regiments usually formed a long, two-man line, with one man kneeling and one man standing behind him. The line was split into groups called platoons. Each platoon was told to fire at a different time so that the line was always defended.

Whether he meant to or not, a man joined the army and took his first day's pay by merely touching the king's shilling. Because of this rule, some men were tricked into 21 years of army service by shaking hands with a soldier who had a shilling hidden in his palm.

IN BATTLE

Private Fell bit off the end of his cartridge (see page 46).

Corporal Naylor put some powder from his cartridge in the pan. He then dropped the rest of the powder, and the ball, down the gun barrel.

Corporal Naylor used his ramrod to push the powder and ball down into the barrel.

The soldiers pulled back the flints and released them, firing the guns.

After firing several times, they charged.

NAPOLEONIC WARS 1799-1815

Private John Green (British) and Sergeant Dominique Courvoisier (French)

Napoleon Bonaparte took control of the French government in 1799. He planned to conquer Europe, India, the Caribbean and the Middle East. In 1804, he proclaimed himself French Emperor and planned to invade Britain. Admiral Nelson defeated Napoleon's navy at the battle of Trafalgar in 1805 and prevented the invasion. In 1808 a British army was sent to Portugal to defend it against the French. This campaign was called the Peninsular War (1808–1814), and by the end, the French army had been driven back to France. Napoleon invaded Russia in 1812, but it was a disaster, with 600,000 soldiers dying, mostly from cold and hunger. In 1814, the British army invaded France, and Napoleon was exiled. He returned in 1815 and raised a new army, which was defeated by British and Prussian forces at Waterloo. John Green *(below)* fought in Spain and France, but by the end of the Napoleonic wars, a veteran French soldier such as Sergeant Courvoisier *(see opposite)* might have served in campaigns all over Europe, as well as in Russia.

ABOVE: *Soldiers were issued with mess tins, but had to provide other personal items themselves.*

The bugle on the shako (hat) is the light infantry's symbol. The regimental colours of the 68th Durham Light Infantry were red and green. Red was a traditional colour for soldiers' jackets, which were made of wool. The lace sewn onto their jacket fronts had red and green thread running through it.

JOINING THE ARMY

John Green enlisted in 1806 because he could not get work as a labourer. His pay – a shilling a day, of which nine pence was kept for expenses – was less than a labourer's, but it was better than starving. John enlisted for seven years, which meant he would not get a pension unless he was wounded (men who joined the army for life got a retirement pension).

John carried a blanket, a knapsack, a water canteen, a ration bag and a cartridge box. Soldiers carrying all this sometimes had to march 60 miles in 24 hours in the hot Spanish sun.

Sergeant Dominique Courvoisier of the 21ième de Ligne (21st Line Infantry).

Dominique's calfskin pack contained his eating equipment, which included a small frying pan and some spare clothes. Napoleon's military tactics depended on having fast-moving armies and as food wagons slowed the army down, soldiers were often not given any rations at all. Instead, they had to find food for themselves.

LEFT: *The gold stripe on Dominique's lower arm shows that he is a sergeant, and the two red chevrons each represent seven years' service.*

NAPOLEON'S ARMY

There were three types of infantry regiments in Napoleon's army: the guards, light infantry and line infantry. Originally the light infantry's role had been to engage in skirmishes (short fights) and keep the enemy busy until the army was ready to attack. But by the time of the Napoleonic Wars, the line infantry, which was the main body of foot soldiers, also contained its own light infantry. Called the *voltigeurs*, they fought side by side with *grenadiers* (the tallest and strongest men) and *fusiliers* (musketeers) like Dominique.

The guards unit were the elite of the army. Their original job was to guard Napoleon, but by 1812 the unit had grown to the size of an army.

Dominique's cartridge box was decorated with an "N" (for Napoleon). He carried a Charleville flintlock musket, and he was allowed to carry a sabre (curved sword) because he was a sergeant. These were called sabres-briquets. *Many soldiers found them useless for fighting but good for chopping up firewood.*

AMERICAN CIVIL WAR 1861-65

Private Rap Lee Cathey (Confederate) and Private Walter Plumb (Union)

In many ways, the American Civil War was the first modern war. It was the first conflict in which messages were sent by telegraph, the first in which troops were transported to battle by train, and the first in which machine guns were used. Over 600,000 people died in the war, making it the bloodiest in American history.

The war started because the Southern states became unhappy with laws imposed on them by President Lincoln's government.

Instead they wanted to govern themselves. The Northern and Southern states had quarrelled over many issues, but the two most important ones were trade and slavery. By early 1861, 11 Southern states had broken away from the Union and formed the Confederated States of America. They formed their own government, elected a president, and set up an army to fight against the Northern states.

ABOVE AND RIGHT: *Sutlers, or military provisioners, sold items like these to the men. Some things, like the "housewife" or sewing set* (shown right) *were useful, but soldiers threw others away when they proved too much to carry on the march.*

MOTIVES

Rap Lee Cathey (*opposite, kneeling*) of the 2nd Virginia Infantry enlisted in April 1861, the first month of the war. Like most Americans, he thought that the war would soon be over, but it soon became clear that the fighting would continue for some time. Rap, like many Confederate soldiers, came from a farming family. Since he did not own slaves himself, Rap was not concerned about preserving slavery, but he did not like people from the North telling him what to do.

Walter Plumb of the 119th New York Volunteers (*opposite, standing*) enlisted in 1862. The army was offering a bounty of $250, and since Walter's wife was expecting a baby, he needed the money. Although some of his fellow soldiers were abolitionists (people who wanted to end slavery), Walter was not concerned about slavery. He thought that the Southern states were insulting the Union and the American flag by trying to break away and govern themselves.

ABOVE: *Knapsack, blanket, tent section, and spare underwear. The Southern states had strong links with England, where they exported a lot of cotton. Some items of Confederate kits, such as this knapsack, were made in England.*

Both armies had good postal systems, and Walter and Rap wrote home regularly.

Rap was tired of coffee made from acorns, so he traded tobacco for proper coffee beans. Tobacco was plentiful in the South, where it was grown, but scarce in the North, and Walter wanted to smoke his pipe. If enemy soldiers were caught trading like this, they would be punished.

FOOD

Union and Confederate soldiers got similar rations: they were mainly meat and "hardtack" biscuits, which had to be soaked overnight in water to soften them enough to eat. Food supplies were often low, either because of shortages or because supply wagons were delayed. If the soldiers were lucky, they received corn, sweet potatoes, and hominy (cracked corn) and black-eyed peas for making porridge. If they were hungry on the march, soldiers would raid the cornfields, orchards and farmyards they passed.

MARCHING AND FIGHTING

Although soldiers sometimes travelled on trains and troopships, they often had to march to battles. Sometimes men went into battle exhausted from marching long distances over dusty or muddy roads.

In the early Civil War battles, the infantry stood and fired at each other in the same way as the infantry did in the American Revolution. Constantly under fire, the infantry would begin to move toward the enemy until they could fight hand-to-hand if necessary. Soldiers were issued with bayonets for close fighting, but it was far more common for them to use the butts of their guns as clubs for hitting their opponents. However, when more powerful guns were introduced, many generals realized that if soldiers were right in the line of fire, thousands of men would get shot for no reason, so they ordered pits and trenches to be dug for the soldiers' protection (see page 35).

CASUALTIES

Wounded men usually received treatment on the battlefield before being sent to makeshift hospitals set up in nearby houses or schools. Anaesthetic was used, but the doctors did not clean their instruments or change their bloodstained clothes between operations. They did

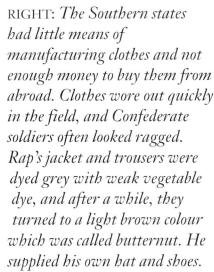

not know that they were spreading germs. For example, wounded limbs were usually amputated and the part left often became infected, killing the patient. More than half of the war casualties were not from injuries but from diseases like dysentery which are caused by germs. There were no proper toilets in the soldiers' camps, and conditions were not much cleaner in the hospitals.

As soldiers like Walter and Rap did not wear identification tags, it was hard to identify dead bodies on the battlefield unless they had letters in their pockets. Before battles, Walter wrote his name on a piece of paper and pinned it to his clothes so that his body could be identified if he was killed. Roll calls were taken after battles, but the army did not always know what had happened to the missing men.

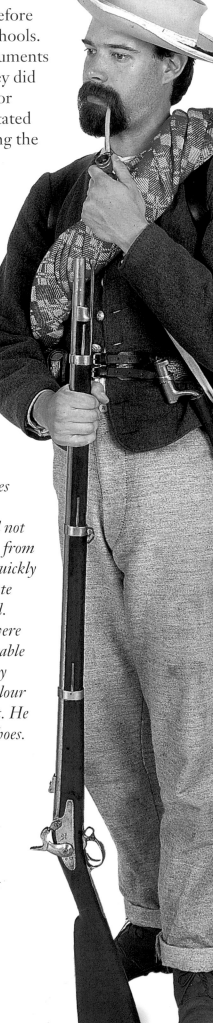

RIGHT: *The Southern states had little means of manufacturing clothes and not enough money to buy them from abroad. Clothes wore out quickly in the field, and Confederate soldiers often looked ragged. Rap's jacket and trousers were dyed grey with weak vegetable dye, and after a while, they turned to a light brown colour which was called butternut. He supplied his own hat and shoes.*

LEFT: *Rap carried a knapsack, wooden water bottle, cartridge box and bayonet. A blanket roll was slung across his shoulder. Beneath the blanket roll he kept a tin pot for making coffee.*

LEFT: *Walter wore a dark blue jacket and sky-blue trousers, both woollen. In winter he wore a blue overcoat (see far right).*

RIGHT: *On his left hip, Walter carried a fabric-covered metal water bottle and a bayonet scabbard. On his back was a knapsack, a rolled-up blanket and a cartridge box.*

FIRING BY FILE

When soldiers were suddenly confronted by the enemy, they stood in two ranks and fired by file. The first two men would fire, then the second two, then the third, and so on down the line.

Emptying the powder and lead ball from the cartridge into the gun's muzzle.

Pushing them down the barrel with the ramrod.

Placing the percussion cap on the nipple.

Firing the guns.

MUSKETS

Although some new weapons were introduced during the Civil War, the chief weapon for both armies was the musket *(see right and below)*, which was produced either by the Springfield armoury in Massachusetts or by the Enfield Company of Great Britain. These had been improved since the time of the American Revolution by adding a percussion cap. This was a small copper cap *(see right)* that fitted over a little knob called the nipple. When the gun was fired, the hammer hit the percussion cap, and the sparks set off the powder inside the gun and fired it.

BELOW: *A musket, bayonet, and cartridge box with cartridges, and a three-pronged tool used to repair the musket. Muskets were now rifled, which meant that there were spiral grooves inside the barrel. These grooves made the ball spin as it flew out of the gun, making it more accurate over a longer distance.*

THE AMERICAN INDIAN WARS 1854-90

Bad Hand (Cheyenne Warrior) and James H. Thomas (Buffalo Soldier)

At the start of the 19th century, American Indian tribes lived on the central plains of North America. Among these tribes, known as Plains Indians, were the Cheyenne, whose territory formed parts of Montana, Wyoming and Colorado. There were 12 main tribes of Plains Indians, including the Sioux, the Blackfoot and the Crow, and they often fought each other in order to capture horses and secure hunting grounds with plenty of buffalo. War was important to them: the way for a man to gain respect was to be brave in battle *(see opposite)*.

White Americans began to claim land in the West in the mid 1800s, and US army forts, often staffed by buffalo soldiers *(see page 31)* were built on the Plains Indians' territory. Misunderstandings between settlers and Plains Indians led to the massacre of a Sioux village, which was the start of more than 30 years of conflict between Plains Indians and the US army. By 1890, the Plains Indians' way of life was destroyed, and the tribes were forced to live in small areas called reservations.

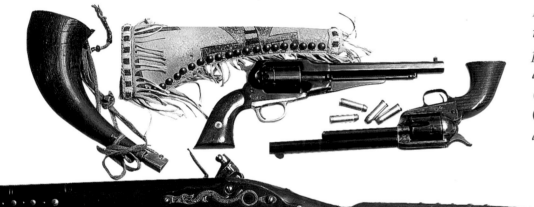

ABOVE: *Items acquired in raids or by trading:* (clockwise from left) *a porcupine-tail brush, a bag made from a cavalryman's boot, a burning glass (magnifying glass) for lighting fires* (see page 18), *tinted glasses, tweezers and a mirror.*

FIGHTING

The Plains Indians did not have an army. When they fought other tribes, only small numbers of men were involved, and what mattered most was the bravery of individual warriors. Their ideas about war did not include military discipline, with soldiers obeying orders, and they had never fought against large numbers of troops like the US army. Traditionally, many tribes were enemies, so different tribes rarely banded together to fight against the army.

The Plains Indians knew they needed guns *(see above left)*, not bows and arrows, to fight the army, and every warrior wanted one. Some of the most common were *(top)* revolvers like the .44 Remington and the .45 Colt, which was used by the US army; *(centre)* the musket; and *(bottom)* the .44 Henry. A decorated holster and a powder horn are also pictured. Guns were often decorated with brass studs.

BELOW: *Bows and arrows were better than guns for hunting buffalo, because they were silent and didn't scare away the animals.*

COUNTING COUP

Men who had gained battle honours or "coups" by displays of bravery were highly respected. Coups could be earned in several ways. The most common was deliberately to touch an enemy – either with the hand or with a weapon or stick held in the hand – without harming him. Taking an enemy's horse or gun was a major coup, but in many tribes, killing an enemy was only a minor coup. Coup marks, like war medals, showed the bravery of the wearer. A warrior of high status had the right to wear a warbonnet, or feathered headdress (see page 30).

Shields were believed to have spiritual and physical power to prevent their owners from being wounded.

Ready for battle. Bad Hand's horse Wapaha (War-bonnet) wore a necklace strung with US army cartridges and scalps. His ears were slit to show that he was a warhorse, and his nostrils were painted red to make him look fierce.

One of the coup marks on Wapaha's legs was red, because Bad Hand was wounded at the time he counted coup.

The American Indian wars were fought on horseback. A good warrior like Bad Hand might have had as many as 25 horses, but only one was strong and brave enough to be a warhorse. The red markings on the horse's body show where he was wounded in previous battles.

Bad Hand wore special clothes for the ceremony before a battle. His warbonnet and ceremonial lance show that he had high status in his tribe.

Bad Hand's sleeves were decorated with hair from enemies killed by his war party. Often, enemies were scalped because hair was considered part of a person's spiritual power and removing it took power away from him.

Leaders of war parties carried pipes. Warriors who smoked the leader's pipe in a pre-battle ceremony accepted his leadership for that battle.

When Bad Hand was 15 he acted as water carrier on his first war party, but by 17 he was considered to be a warrior. When he reached 40, he stopped going to war because he had gained enough coups to have high status in the tribe.

MEDICINE

American Indians believed that everything in the world was part of one Great Spirit and was a source of spiritual power which was called "medicine". There were many kinds of medicine: the sun, moon and sky all had special power. Medicine protected warriors in battle. It was acquired in visions – for example, Bad Hand painted his shield with symbols from his dreams so that he would not get killed in battle.

LEFT: *A buffalo robe with a pictogram of a battle, with (clockwise from left) bags of red and yellow war paint; a tobacco twist, pouch and pipe; an arrow for pressing down the tobacco in the pipe; a buffalo shoulder-bone board for cutting tobacco and sacred herbs.*

BUFFALO SOLDIERS

When the government realized that extra soldiers were needed to fight in the Indian wars, new regiments were formed. They were commanded by white officers but made up entirely of black soldiers. The American Indians called these men buffalo soldiers because they thought their hair looked like the thick coat of the buffalo.

Although slavery had been ended by the Civil War, racist laws and attitudes meant that black men like James H. Thomas had little chance of education and few career opportunities. To James, the army offered education, a career, and a retirement pension. Soldiers enlisted for five years, and black regiments had the highest re-enlistment rate in the army and the lowest desertion rate. The pay was low, but black and white soldiers received the same amount of money.

Buffalo soldiers like James served from the Canadian to the Mexican borders of America. They were usually stationed at forts, living in barracks. When they were not in combat, they helped to build frontier forts and put up telegraph lines.

ABOVE: *Within ten years of joining the army, James H. Thomas had been promoted to Quartermaster Sergeant, the highest rank a black soldier could hold. Quartermaster Sergeants made sure that the soldiers had the right equipment. The job involved a lot of paper-work and could only be done by an educated man.*

EQUIPMENT

The government outfitted new regiments in left-over Civil War uniforms *(see page 26)*. Soldiers had white gloves which they wore to collect their pay. They were issued Springfield "trap door" rifles *(see right)*. These were Civil War muzzle-loading guns that had been changed into breech-loaders *(see page 46)*. At this time, it was against the law for a black civilian to own a gun.

Arthur always carried his pay book, which recorded the details of his army service and how much he was paid. If he was killed, it would help to identify his body. Soldiers could choose to have some of their pay sent home to their families.

Arthur's pack weighed 70 lbs when it was full. His mess kit, in a cloth cover, hung on the outside of his pack.

Arthur was issued this leather jerkin the first winter that he was in the trenches, to help him keep warm.

The diagonal band on Arthur's cuff was a good-conduct stripe. Below it, he had a metal wound stripe. Arthur's wound was a "blighty one" – it was severe enough for him to be sent back to England for treatment. When it healed, he was ordered back to the trenches to continue fighting.

FIRST WORLD WAR 1914-18

British, German, French, American and Australian Soldiers

Before World War I, the three great powers of Western Europe – Britain, France and Germany – were competing to be the strongest country with the largest empire. In eastern Europe, there were two vast empires: Russia and Austria-Hungary. These five nations formed two alliances: Germany and Austria-Hungary on one side, called the Central Powers; and France, Britain, and Russia on the other, called the Allies.

Germany planned to declare war on France, defeat it, and then attack Russia, which had a larger army. But when the Germans marched into Belgium, the British, who had promised to help if Belgium was invaded, declared war on Germany.

When war broke out, Arthur Fisher, like many other British men, volunteered. They were eager to fight for their king, George V, and country, and were afraid that if they delayed, they might miss the war, as everyone in Britain thought that Germany would soon be defeated and that the war would probably be "over by Christmas". Arthur left his job to enlist, and after training, he was sent to the Western Front, which ran through Belgium and France.

Although Arthur was used to trench life (see page 35), he hated being unwashed and having lice. Arthur burnt the louse eggs in his clothes with a candle and squashed the adult lice, but it only took a few days before he started to itch again.

ABOVE: *The wooden stick is the handle of Arthur's entrenching tool. The other part was carried in the leather pouch slung below his pack. Joined together, the two parts made a shovel for digging trenches.*

BELOW: *Short magazine Lee Enfield rifle. A trained soldier could fire more than 15 aimed bullets per minute. Arthur fixed his bayonet to the end of his rifle when he advanced across No-man's-land with the other soldiers to attack the enemy.*

TRENCH WARFARE

The method of fighting used on the Western Front was called trench warfare. Trenches were long, narrow ditches dug about ten feet deep. British and French trenches stretched across France and Belgium, often only a few metres away from the German trenches. The land between the enemy trenches was called no-man's-land.

If the generals decided to attack, the artillery would fire thousands of shells across no-man's-land to try to kill as many of the enemy as possible. The soldiers were then told to assemble in one part of the trench, and when the signal was given, they had to scramble out and run across no-man's-land as fast as they could to try to capture the enemy trenches. As they ran, the enemy fired at them. During these attacks, thousands of soldiers were killed in a few minutes.

Besides artillery and machine-gun fire, soldiers were also killed by poisonous gas. The attacking soldiers opened up gas cylinders, and the wind blew the gas towards the enemy trench. If the wind blew in the wrong direction, the attackers might end up gassing themselves. Gas blinded, burnt and killed soldiers.

LEFT: *Early gas masks were chemical-soaked cloth bags* (top, centre), *which did not work well. Later ones* (below) *had air filters.*

FOOD
Arthur's mess kit and food rations. Rations consisted of bully beef (corned beef) and hard biscuits. Rations also included tins of stew, which often had to be eaten cold, and tea, which was brewed behind the lines by army cooks and brought up to the trenches in big vats. The kit roll shown here contains Arthur's knife, fork, and spoon, his razor and shaving brush, and comb.

A British trench store containing tinned food and a "Tommy's cooker". The big jar is full of rum, which was given to soldiers in cold weather or before an attack.

RAIDING PARTY

Sometimes at night, small bands of soldiers went on raiding parties to the enemy trenches to get information about what they were planning to do next. They cut through the barbed wire in no-man's-land with wire cutters like the ones shown *(left)*. Raiding parties were very dangerous, and the soldiers who took part in them were usually volunteers.

LEFT: *British entrenching tool (see page 33), wire cutters and a rattle, which was used to warn the men to put on their masks when there was a gas attack.*

RIGHT: *German Musketier (Musketeer) Kasmir Heska of the 63rd Infantry Regiment, carrying his Mauser 7.92mm calibre rifle. When the war started, Kasmir was an army reservist, which meant that he had done military service and could be called up if Germany went to war. France also used reservists, but Britain relied on volunteers until 1916, when the government introduced conscription.*

TRENCH LIFE

Soldiers like Arthur and Kasmir spent more time digging and repairing trenches than fighting. Heavy rain and continuous shelling turned large areas of France and Belgium into a swamp, full of water-filled craters. All the soldiers found the trenches very uncomfortable places to live because they were muddy and smelly, with nowhere to wash and little food. It was not unusual for soldiers to be up to their knees in water, and there were no proper toilets. In some places, unburied and rotting dead soldiers lying on the ground beside the trench made it stink and caused the spread of disease. Soldiers were normally in the trenches for less than a week at a time, before being sent back to safer areas behind the lines for one or two weeks to rest, train and prepare for another turn in the trenches.

CASUALTIES

Every soldier carried a field dressing to try to stop the bleeding if he was wounded. Wounded men often took refuge in shell craters, but they might have a long and agonizing wait before a stretcher party reached them. If many men were wounded, stretcher parties were told to bring back only those who had a chance of recovery.

Kasmir rolled his blanket up inside a tent section and fastened it across his shoulder. To make a two-man tent, he put his section together with another soldier's.

LEFT: *Kasmir fixed his bayonet to his rifle, and, wearing his helmet, which was painted in "dazzle" camouflage, he went over the top. Soldiers on both sides did a lot of bayonet practice during training, but most casualties were caused not by bayonets, but by artillery, rifle fire or gas.*

ATTRITION

By 1916, generals on both sides could see that the war was not going to end by one side winning a definite victory over the other in battle. As a result of this, they decided that the soldiers should not give up any ground, no matter how many were killed but they should try to wear down the enemy with constant attacks. This tactic is called attrition. Although the generals knew that many of their men would die in this process, they believed that, as long as the enemy lost more men than they did, they would eventually win the war.

By this time, ordinary soldiers like Arthur Fisher no longer thought that the war would be over quickly. Arthur wondered if he would have to carry on fighting until he was an old man, unless he was killed first – all the pals (friends) who had joined the army with him were dead.

In the trench opposite Arthur's, Kasmir spent many nights trying not to listen to the cries of the wounded men lying a few metres away in no-man's-land. Kasmir and the other soldiers wanted to rescue them, but they knew that they would be shot by British or French soldiers if they climbed out of their trench.

LEFT AND BELOW: *Leon Pierre Marie, 2nd class private, of the French army. Unlike other soldiers, French soldiers wore a coat instead of a tunic. The colour of his uniform was horizon blue, and he carried a Lebel rifle.*

RIGHT: *US Staff Sergeant John J. Hincky carried a Springfield rifle.*

ABOVE: *American soldiers in the First World War were called "doughboys" because they said that their packs looked like lumps of dough and would be as useless as lumps of dough on a battlefield!*

GALLIPOLI

Although most of the fighting in World War I took place in Europe, there was also action in Turkey, the Middle East, Africa and China. Turkey joined the Central Powers in November 1914 *(see page 33)*. By 1915, the British commanders had formed a plan to attack Germany through the Balkans. In April 1915, Allied troops, mainly from the Australian and New Zealand Army Corps (ANZACs), landed at Gallipoli. The attack was unsuccessful because Turkish troops on the cliffs above the beach made it impossible for the Allies to move anywhere without heavy losses. It turned into trench warfare, which was made worse by hot weather and outbreaks of cholera and malaria. By October 1915, when most of the Allies withdrew, about 36,000 soldiers had been killed.

Australian uniforms, designed for the battlefield rather than the parade ground, were more comfortable than British ones.

THE END OF THE WAR

America had supplied the Allies with weapons since the war began, but many Americans felt that they should not fight, even though the German U-boats (submarines) were sinking their ships.

In January 1917, British Naval Intelligence de-coded a telegram from Germany offering Mexico the return of Texas, New Mexico and Arizona if it would fight against America. America declared war on Germany in April 1917. Although regular American soldiers were sent to France immediately, it took a year to train volunteers like John Hincky *(see opposite)*, who did not arrive in Europe until early 1918. America had large numbers of men to send to the war, and German manpower and supplies were running short. With America's help, the Allies broke through the German lines, and some German soldiers refused to go on fighting. On November 11 1918, Germany signed an armistice, agreeing to stop fighting and discuss peace.

George Hayward is wearing a slouch hat. These were given to ANZAC troops to wear in hot climates. After Gallipoli, George's unit fought on the Western Front, and he was given a steel helmet to replace his hat.

Private George Hayward of the 4th Battalion Australian Imperial Force. George volunteered because he wanted to help defend the British Empire.

Infantrymen at Gallipoli often wore scraps of white cloth to help the commanders see how the attack had advanced. It was also important for the artillerymen to be able to see the infantry clearly so that they would not fire at them by mistake.

American soldiers were called GIs. The initials stood for General Issue.

American uniforms were olive drab. German ones were field grey.

SECOND WORLD WAR 1939-45

German, American, French, British, Russian and Japanese Soldiers

Unlike previous wars, the Second World War was total war, involving both soldiers and civilians. Fighting took place almost everywhere in the world, and of the 55 million who died, around 30 million were civilians.

The war broke out in September 1939 when Adolf Hitler, the German leader, ordered his army to invade Poland. They used a new type of warfare called *blitzkrieg* (lightning war), sending in tanks and aircraft to break through the Polish defences.

When Hitler refused to withdraw his troops from Poland, Britain, France, Australia, New Zealand and India (called the Allies) declared war on Germany. The Soviet Union (Russia) joined the Allies in June 1941, after Hitler's troops had marched across the Russian border. Both Italy and Japan made alliances with Germany, and these three countries were called the Axis. America joined the Allies in December 1941, after the Japanese attacked the US airbase at Pearl Harbor.

ABOVE: Yank *magazine was produced in America for soldiers fighting abroad.*

LEFT: *Frederick surrendered to GI Norman (see below). Norman looked at Frederick's* Soldbuch *(pay book) to check his identity before handing him over to the military police. Frederick was sent to a prisoner of war (POW) camp in America until the war was over.*

ABOVE: *This German machine gun with its ammunition belt and boxes is an MG 34. MG stands for* Maschinengewehr *(machine gun).*

CONSCRIPTS AND VOLUNTEERS

Frederick Gockel was a student in Hanover, Germany, when he received his call-up papers in the winter of 1944. After basic training, he was sent to one of the new Volksgrenadier divisions, which Hitler intended to use in his attack against the Americans in the Ardennes, Belgium. Although this attack was successful to begin with, by January 1945, the Americans, with their greater manpower, had halted it.

Frederick was taken prisoner by Private Norman Padgett of the US 4th Infantry Division. When the war started in Europe, Norman, who was a salesman, thought that the Americans should not become involved in it, but when he heard about the attack on Pearl Harbor, he volunteered for the army immediately. He thought he would be sent to fight the Japanese and was surprised when he ended up in Europe instead.

THE WAR IN EUROPE

William Linton (*see below*) was called up in April 1940. In May, the Germans invaded Norway, Denmark, the Netherlands and Luxembourg, before marching through Belgium to invade France. William, who worked in a department store, was eager to "do his bit", as his father had done in the First World War.

Like the Poles in 1939, the French army of 1940 was not prepared for the German attack, and northern France was soon under German occupation. The British Expeditionary Force (BEF), which had been sent to France in 1939, became trapped in northern France by the advancing German forces. The BEF and other Allied soldiers, including Pierre Blanc (*see below*), had to be rescued from the beaches of Dunkirk and brought back to England by a variety of boats which ranged from warships to yachts.

In June, the French head of state Marshal Pétain signed an armistice with Germany. Although his government co-operated with the Germans, many French people joined the resistance movement known as the *Maquis*, which helped in the fight against Germany. Pierre Blanc joined the "Free French", a group of soldiers led by General Charles de Gaulle, who were based in England. They refused to accept the armistice signed by Pétain, and continued to fight.

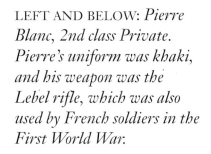

LEFT AND BELOW: *Pierre Blanc, 2nd class Private. Pierre's uniform was khaki, and his weapon was the Lebel rifle, which was also used by French soldiers in the First World War.*

RIGHT: *Private William Linton. William was called up in 1940, just before the Germans invaded France.*

BOMBING

William was worried about the safety of his family, who lived in London and were in danger from German air raids. By 1939, aeroplane technology had greatly improved since the First World War, and all the major powers had air forces. Often, soldiers fighting abroad were in less danger than their families at home. As well as dropping bombs on both military and civilian targets, aeroplanes were used in air battles such as the Battle of Britain (1940).

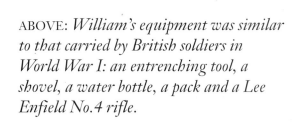

ABOVE: *William's equipment was similar to that carried by British soldiers in World War I: an entrenching tool, a shovel, a water bottle, a pack and a Lee Enfield No.4 rifle.*

PERSONAL KIT

William and the others soldiers were issued with mess tins and kit for washing and shaving. Soldiers who took part in the D-Day invasion were given a French guidebook and French money. British soldiers wore identity disks around their necks. These were marked with the soldier's name, rank, army number and religion.

D-DAY

By June 1940, the Allies began making plans to free the German-occupied European countries, and by 1944, Britain was full of Allied sailors, airmen, and soldiers, including William Linton, who were waiting to invade France on D-Day, June 6. The date was kept secret, and the Germans were taken by surprise. William was very nervous and he and the other soldiers waited for the attack to begin, but he hoped that this invasion might finally beat Hitler. He was right – although the Germans counter-attacked, the D-Day landings led to the overthrow of the Germans in Paris and the capture of Berlin. On May 7 1945, Germany surrendered. May 8 was declared VE (Victory in Europe) Day.

LEFT: *Private Linton is wearing woollen khaki-coloured battle fatigues, a steel helmet with a camouflage cover, and hobnail boots.*

ABOVE: *All soldiers had first-aid training and carried field dressings like these.*

RIGHT: *The Bren gun (top) was the light machine gun used by British soldiers. It fired 500 rounds per minute. The Sten submachine gun (bottom) was also widely used.*

THE EASTERN FRONT

In June 1941, while the war in Europe continued, Hitler invaded the Soviet Union. At first, the invading German army, supported by *Panzer* (tank) divisions and the *Luftwaffe* (air force), made fast progress. However, winter began before the Germans arrived in Moscow, and although the troops came within 19 miles of the city, the very cold weather and strong Russian defences prevented them from capturing it.

Fighting continued in the Soviet Union, especially around the cities of Stalingrad and Leningrad, both of which were besieged by the Germans. The assault on Stalingrad took place in August 1942. Although the Germans moved easily through the city's outskirts, the Russians defended every building in the centre, forcing the Germans to fight from house to house. While this was happening, a Soviet counter-attacking force gathered outside the city. They bombarded the German army until it surrendered in January 1943. The Allies were delighted to hear the news because it showed that the German army was not, as they had begun to think, unbeatable.

The siege of Leningrad lasted from September 1941 until January 1944, during which time about one million people in the city died from starvation and disease. Afterwards, the city was given the title "Hero City" because its inhabitants had defended it so bravely.

RIGHT: *Soviet Army Sergeant Vassili Valentinov. When the Soviets were attacking, the well-trained tank and artillery divisions broke through the enemy lines, followed by huge numbers of infantrymen, who killed as many of the enemy as they could.*

US Marines (see opposite) used Thompson sub-machine guns, known as "Tommy guns". American helmets had the special feature of a fibre lining, which could be removed. The helmet could then be filled with water for washing and shaving if necessary.

Vassili had a PPSh-41 submachine gun. PP stands for pistolet pulyemet, *meaning machine pistol.*

LEFT: *Soviet infantry soldiers were often badly trained and undisciplined. They sometimes went for as long as three weeks without receiving rations, and they had to live off the land. When the supplies arrived, there was a ration of vodka as well as food.*

THE WAR IN THE PACIFIC

The war was also being fought on the other side of the world. In December 1941 the Japanese attacked two British colonies, Malaya (now Malaysia) and Hong Kong. They also launched a surprise attack on the Pearl Harbor US naval base. The United States and Britain immediately declared war on Japan. At first, Japanese forces controlled the Pacific, and they soon occupied many of its islands and invaded Burma. Japanese expansion was halted after defeats by the US navy, and US forces began to recapture the islands. The Pacific war ended when the US air force dropped atomic bombs on Hiroshima and Nagasaki (August 6 and 9 1945). Japan surrendered on August 14, and the next day was declared VJ (Victory over Japan) Day.

Richard Mawson (*below*) was 19 when he joined the Marines. He expected that fighting in the Pacific would be tough, but he was unprepared for the sight of his buddies (friends) being mown down by machine gun fire, or for the rotting corpses that lay next to his "foxhole".

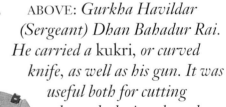

Private Richard Mawson, 4th US Marine Division. He wore a thin cotton uniform, specially designed for fighting in hot countries, and a helmet with a camouflage cover. Around his neck he wore "dog tags", to identify him if he was killed.

ABOVE: *Gurkha Havildar (Sergeant) Dhan Bahadur Rai. He carried a* kukri, *or curved knife, as well as his gun. It was useful both for cutting through the jungle and as a weapon. Gurkhas, who were recruited into the British army from Nepal, served in Burma, which meant enduring a hot climate, dense jungle, tropical diseases and months of continual rain.*

LEFT: *Japanese Private First Class Renya Toyodo, in winter uniform. Renya was proud to be serving Emperor Hirohito. Hirohito had the status of a god, and soldiers considered it an honour to sacrifice their lives for him.*

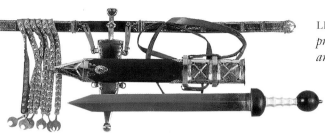

LEFT: *Roman soldier's belt with protective bronze apron, sword and dagger*

RIGHT: *Sergeant Richard Laird, American soldier in the American War of Independence*

TIME LINE

509 BC	• Rome becomes a republic
58–51 BC	• Julius Caesar conquers Gaul
43 BC	• Claudius conquers Britain
c.122 AD	• Hadrian's Wall is built in Northern Britain
	• Roman Empire is at its height
476 AD	• Last Roman Emperor deposed
800–1100	• Viking raids on Europe: Vikings settle in Britain and France
1066	✗ Hastings
	• Duke William of Normandy is crowned William I
1096–99	• First Crusade
1147–49	• Second Crusade
1187	• Muslims recapture Jerusalem
1191–92	• Third Crusade
1202–04	• Fourth Crusade

1337–1453	**Hundred Years War**
c.1340	• Cannon first in use
c.1380	• Handguns first in use

RIGHT: *William Trussel, crusader*

1455–85	**Wars of The Roses**
	Important events:
1460	✗ Northampton, Wakefield
1469	✗ Edgecote
1471	✗ Barnet
1485	✗ Bosworth
1500	• Wheel-lock mechanism first fitted on handguns
1642–49	**English Civil War**
	Important events:
1642	✗ Edgehill
1644	✗ Marston Moor
1645	✗ Naseby
1649	• Execution of Charles I
c.1650–1700	• European armies adopt guns with flintlock mechanism
c.1650	• Bayonet invented in Bayonne, France
c.1700	• Bayonet in general use

1775–83	**American Revolution**
	Important events:
1775	✗ Lexington, Concord, Bunker Hill
1776	✗ Trenton
1777	✗ Saratoga
1780	✗ Charleston
1781	✗ Yorktown
1799–1815	**Napoleonic Wars**
	Important events:
1805	✗ Trafalgar
1808–14	Peninsular War
1812	• Napoleon invades Russia
1815	✗ Waterloo
1832	• American Samuel Colt patents design for revolver

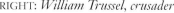

LEFT: *Bible, bullets, American Civil War*

RIGHT: *Sergeant Elsie Pannell, British Auxiliary Territorial Services, Second World War*

1861–65	**American Civil War**
	Important events:
1861	✗ First Bull Run (Manassas)
1862	✗ Antietam
1862	✗ Shiloh
1863	✗ Gettysburg
1862	• American Richard Gatling patents first machine gun
1864	• The Red Cross Society founded to care for war casualties
1867	• Swedish Alfred Nobel manufactures the explosive dynamite
1854–90	**American Indian Wars**
	Important events:
1876	✗ Little Big Horn
1890	✗ Wounded Knee
1867	• Barbed wire patented
1882	• Field telephones first in use
1883	• American inventor Hiram Maxim introduces the first fully automatic machine gun
1903	• American Wright brothers make the first powered aircraft flight

1914–18	**First World War**
	Important events:
1914	✗ The Marne
	• German invasion of France halted
April 1915	• German army uses gas for first time at Ypres. By September, the Allies are using gas
1915	• The Gallipoli campaign
1916	✗ Verdun
1916	✗ The Somme
	• Tanks are used for the first time, by the British army
1917	✗ Passchendaele (Third Battle of Ypres)
	• USA joins the Allies
1918	• Armistice Day (November 11th)

LEFT: *Bad Hand, Cheyenne warrior, American Indian Wars*

1939–45	**Second World War**
	Important events:
1940	• Dunkirk evacuation of France
	• Battle of Britain
1941	• Germans invade USSR
	• Pearl Harbor
	• USA joins Allies
	• British women are conscripted for the first time. They join the Auxiliary Services, or work on farms or in weapons' factories
1942	✗ El Alamein
	✗ Coral Sea and Midway
1944	• D-Day (June 6th)
1945	• Allies invade Germany
	• VE (Victory in Europe) Day (May 8th)
	• Major US air offensive against Japan
	• American flyers drop atomic bombs on Hiroshima and Nagasaki
	• VJ (Victory in Japan) Day (August 15th)

GLOSSARY

Artillery Originally, an artillery piece was a weapon that fired heavy missiles, such as large cannon balls. The word artillery is now used to describe any gun of higher calibre (see below) than a machine gun.

Auxiliary A soldier who has a supporting role. Auxiliaries in the Roman army supported the legionaries by skirmishing with the enemy until the army was ready to attack. Female soldiers in the British Auxiliary Territorial Service in the Second World War supported the male soldiers, but were not allowed to fire guns themselves. Auxiliary soldiers are sometimes mercenaries (see below) in the service of a foreign government.

Barracks A building or group of buildings lived in by soldiers.

Barrel The tubular part of a gun, from which the bullet or shell is fired.

Bayonet A short, stabbing blade which can be fixed onto the muzzle of a musket or rifle.

Bombardment A prolonged and intense attack using artillery (see above).

Breech-loader Any firearm in which the shell or bullet is loaded from behind the barrel, as opposed to a muzzle-loader (see below).

Calibre The diameter of a shell or bullet. For example, British rifles and machine guns in the First and Second World Wars used .303 inch calibre ammunition.

Camouflage A disguise using paint or parts of natural things such as leaves and branches, so that soldiers can blend in with the surroundings and not be spotted by the enemy.

Cartridge A tubular case made of metal or paper which contains the explosive charge for a weapon. It usually contains the shell or bullet as well.

Conscription Compulsory military service. Conscripts are men (and occasionally women) who have been ordered to join the army. This often happens when a country is involved in a conflict – for example, there was conscription in Great Britain during the Second World War.

Crusade Any war that is fought for a religious cause – the term crusade particularly refers to military expeditions to the Holy Land made in the 11th, 12th and 13th centuries in order to capture the city of Jerusalem and the land surrounding it from the Muslims.

Enlisting Joining the army. Men originally wrote down their names, or, if they could not write, put a "mark" on a list to show that they had joined.

File A line of soldiers standing one behind the other.

Lace Coloured tape or braiding on soldiers' uniforms which identifies the regiment in which they serve.

Machine gun An automatic weapon which is capable of continuous fire. Early machine guns were heavy and difficult to move around, and during the First World War the light or submachine gun, which could be carried by one man, was introduced.

Mail An early form of armour made from interlocking rings of metal.

Mercenary A soldier hired to fight for a foreign army, who fights for money, rather than loyalty to that particular country or ruler.

Mess This term was originally used to refer to a meal eaten by a group of soldiers, but it is also used to refer to both the soldiers' eating place and to a group of soldiers who normally eat together (known as messmates).

Militia An army made up of civilians who are not full-time soldiers, but who have enlisted to serve only during emergencies.

Musket A long barrelled, muzzle-loading gun.

Muzzle-loader Any firearm in which the shell or bullet is loaded from the front end of the barrel, or muzzle.

Pan Pan-shaped area at the breech of a muzzle-loading gun where a small amount of priming powder is placed to ignite the main charge in the barrel and cause the gun to fire.

Pike A spearhead fixed to a pole of up to 21 feet in length.

Pistol A handgun, usually with a short barrel.

Priming powder Fine gunpowder which is placed in the pan of a musket to set off the main charge in the barrel.

Ramrod A long wooden or metal pole which is used to push the bullet down the barrel of a muzzle-loader.

Rank A line of soldiers standing side by side. The term rank also refers to a soldier's position within the army (eg, sergeant, corporal).

Regiment A military unit consisting of between 800 to 1,200 soldiers.

Revolver A firearm with revolving chambers inside, which allows several bullets to be loaded at once, so that the gun can be fired repeatedly without re-loading.

Rifle A long-barrelled firearm with spiral grooves inside the barrel, which make the bullet or shell spin as it is shot out of the gun. This makes the gun more accurate over a longer range.

Saltpetre Another name for the chemical compound potassium nitrate, which is used in gunpowder.

INDEX

PLACES TO VISIT

Military re-enactments and events are held at various English Heritage properties during the summer months. For information and details of events, telephone 0171 – 973 3396.

American Museum
Claverton Manor, Bath,
Avon BA2 7BD
01225 – 460503
American history

Basing House
Basingstoke, Hants RG24 7HB
01256 – 467294
Civil War battle site

Battle Abbey
Battle, East Sussex TN33 OAD
01424 – 773792
English Heritage
Battlefield and remains of church built by William the Conqueror

Carlisle Castle
Carlisle, Cumbria CA3 8UR
01228 – 591922
English Heritage
Norman castle

Chester's Roman Fort and Museum
Chollerford, Humshaugh, Hexham,
Northumberland NA46 4EP
01434 – 681379
English Heritage
Roman fort near Hadrian's Wall

Dartmouth Castle
Dartmouth, Devon TQ6 OJN
01803 – 833588
English Heritage
Fifteenth-century castle with Victorian coastal defence battery

Dover Castle and Hellfire Corner
Dover, Kent CT16 1HH
01304 – 201628
English Heritage
Castle with military history from the Iron Age to the Second World War

Durham Light Infantry Museum
Aykley Heads, Durham City,
County Durham DH1 5TU
01385 – 42214
Two hundred years of regimental history

Eden Camp Modern History
Theme Museum
Eden Camp, Malton,
N. Yorkshire YO17 OSD
01653 – 697777
Second World War exhibition

Framlingham Castle
Framlingham, Woodbridge,
Suffolk IP13 9BP
01728 – 724189
English Heritage
Medieval castle

Gurkha Museum
Penninsula Barracks, Romsey Road,
Winchester, Hants. SO23 8TS
01962 – 842832
Regimental history

Imperial War Museum
Lambeth Road, London SE1 6HZ
0171 – 416 5000
First and Second World War exhibitions

Kenilworth Castle
Warwickshire CV8 1NE
01926 – 852078
English Heritage
Norman keep

National Army Museum
Royal Hospital Road, Chelsea,
London SW3 4HT
0171 – 730 0717
Five hundred years of British soldiers

Pendennis Castle
Falmouth, Cornwall TR11 5LP
01326 – 316594
English Heritage
Built by Henry VIII for coastal defence

Royal Army Medical Corps Historical
Museum
Keogh Barracks, Ash Vale, Aldershot,
Hants. GU12 5RQ
01252 – 340212
History of military medicine

Royal Armouries Museum
Armouries Drive, Leeds LS10 1LT
0113 – 220 1999
Historical collection of arms and armour

Tower of London
Tower Hill, London EC4N 4AB
0171 – 709 0765
Historical collection of arms and armour

ACKNOWLEDGEMENTS

Breslich & Foss would like to thank the following people for sharing their enthusiasm with us, for allowing themselves to be photographed, for lending us equipment and for answering our questions so patiently:

pp4–5 Chris Haines, Tony Segalini and Richard Story of the Ermine Street Guard

pp6–7 Roland Williamson of *Regalia Anglorum*

pp8–11 John Cole, John Jay Phillips, David Page and Ian Jeremish of Conquest

pp12–13 Ian Pycroft, Mark Griffin and Philip Allen of the Merchant's House

pp14–17 Alan Turton, Simon Frame and Thomas Gray of the English Civil War Society

pp18–19 Edmund Moderacki, James P. Sieradzki and James Boswell of the Brigade of the American Revolution; Richard Patterson of the Old Barracks Museum, Trenton, New Jersey

pp20–21 Gary Brierley and Alan McEwan of the 47th Regiment of Foot

pp22–23 Sean Phillips and Ian Miller of the 68th Regt. Durham Light Infantry, Mr and Mrs Phillips, and Michael Rimmer; Mike Freeman and Richard Ransome of the *21ième Regiment d'Infanterie de ligne*

pp24–27 Chris Shreiber, Sam Cathey and Christopher Daley of the American Civil War Society

pp28–31 Michael Terry, Joe and Jean Brandl and David Jurgella; William Gwaltney of Fort Laramie, Wyoming, and Andrew Maisich of the Colorado History Museum. Photographs on p. 31 appear courtesy of the Colorado Historical Society

pp32–43 Trevor Poole and Tom Hill of the Great War Society; Mike Barnes, Titus, Michael Johnson, Maurice Stokes; Robert Stedman, Martin Brayley, Laurent Ladrosse, Richard Ingram, Simon Vanlint, Tim Sparks and Jumkaji Gurung; Gerard Gorokhoff, Phillipe Charbonnier, Brigadier Bullock of the Gurkha Museum, Andrew Fletcher of BAPTY and Nick Hall of Sabre Sales, 85 Castle Road, Southsea.

p45 Isabelle Campion

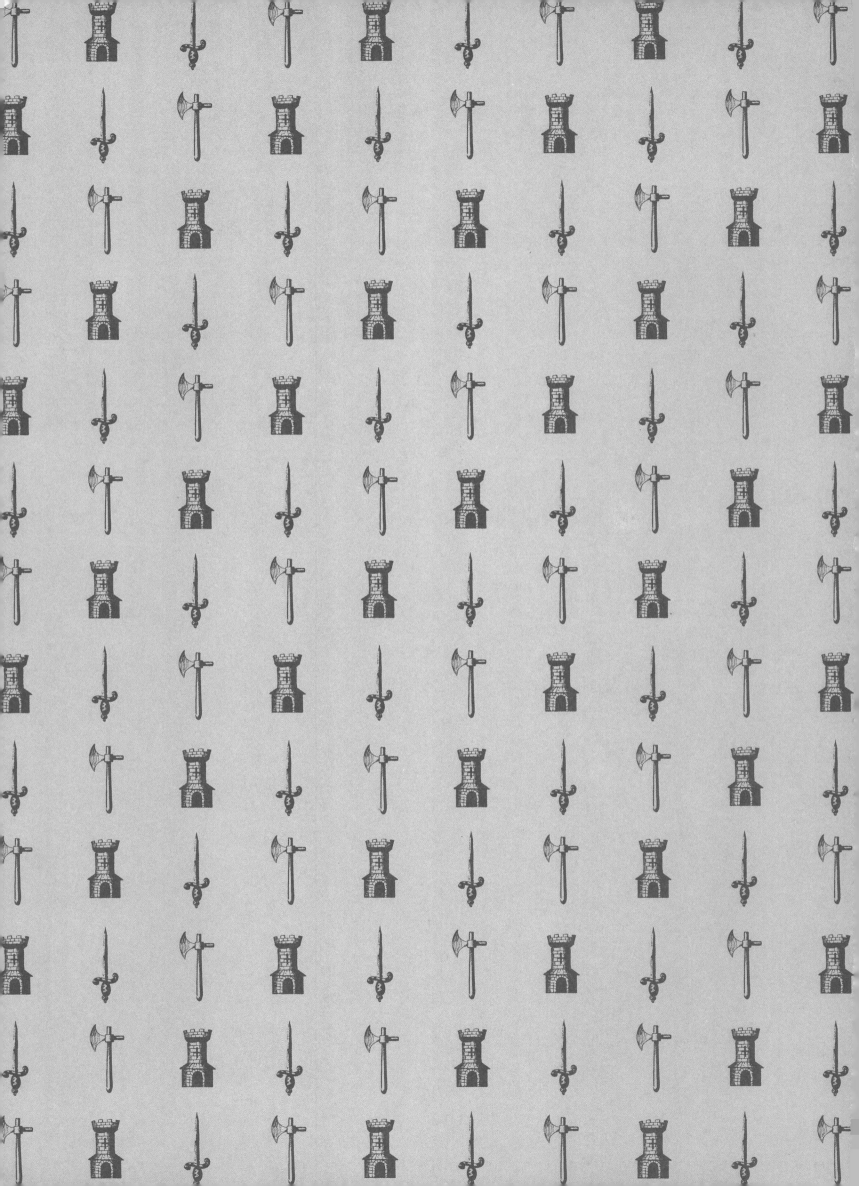